R. F. Dearborn

Saratoga and How to See It

R. F. Dearborn

Saratoga and How to See It

ISBN/EAN: 9783337417710

Printed in Europe, USA, Canada, Australia, Japan

Cover: Foto ©Andreas Hilbeck / pixelio.de

More available books at **www.hansebooks.com**

CONTAINING A FULL ACCOUNT OF ITS

MINERAL SPRINGS

AND

ATTRACTIONS,

WITH NUMEROUS ILLUSTRATIONS.

Published by R. F. Dearborn, and

FOR SALE BY THE AMERICAN NEWS CO.,

115, 117, 119 & 121 NASSAU ST., N. Y.,

ALBANY NEWS CO., ALBANY, Etc., Etc.

Waverly House

SARATOGA, N. Y.

The Hotel is substantially built of brick, and is fire-proof, nearly new, has recently been refitted and repainted, and will be in first-class order throughout. It is beautifully shaded with trees, and has a two-story piazza for promenade extending 340 feet, with ample pleasure grounds adjoining, and is unequaled in its attractions and advantages as a summer resort for families; while its location on Broadway is unsurpassed by any Hotel in Saratoga for beauty, convenience and comfort, and being in close proximity to all the most celebrated Springs.

The *Parlors* and *Sleeping Rooms* are all large, well ventilated, well furnished and pleasant. The *Tables* will be liberally supplied with every delicacy of the season.

Carriages will be awaiting the arrival of every train to convey visitors to and from the Hotel free of charge. A livery is connected with the establishment and abundant stable room for those desiring their own teams.

TERMS REASONABLE.

All correspondence promptly answered and full information cheerfully given.

WILLIAM C. JONES,

Proprietor.

SARATOGA,

AND

HOW TO SEE IT:

CONTAINING A FULL ACCOUNT OF ITS

CELEBRATED SPRINGS, MAMMOTH HOTELS,

HEALTH INSTITUTIONS,

BEAUTIFUL DRIVES AND WALKS,

VARIOUS OBJECTS OF INTEREST AND AMUSEMENT,

WITH THE

ARRIVAL AND DEPARTURE OF TRAINS,

FARE AND DISTANCE TO VARIOUS PLACES,

A COMPLETE LIST OF THE

HOTELS AND PRINCIPAL BOARDING HOUSES,

&c., &c., &c.,

With NUMEROUS ILLUSTRATIONS and a

MAP OF SARATOGA SPRINGS.

SARATOGA, N. Y.:

R. F. DEARBORN,

1871.

WEED, PARSONS AND COMPANY, PRINTERS, ALBANY, N. Y.

CONTENTS.

SARATOGA AND HOW TO SEE IT.

INTRODUCTION.

SARATOGA, for a long time the most fashionable watering place in the world, is still increasing in reputation and popularity every year.

Its wonderful mineral springs, so diverse in their constituents and medical properties, have continued to send forth their healing waters of unimpaired strength, while others of equal virtue and more varied composition, flowing from newly developed fountains, are increasing the wide range of their adaptation. Within a few years so many changes have occurred by the retubing of old springs and the discovery of several new ones, that strangers and invalids are more than ever perplexed to know the peculiarities of each, and the one specially adapted to their necessities. When the waters should be drank, how often and how much, are questions of interest to every visitor.

To supply the information so many desire in regard to the springs, and to place before every visitor to Saratoga, in a few words and at a moderate price, an account of its attractions and advantages, is the object of this little pamphlet. We have endeavored to make the work impartial and reliable, and without fear or favor, and, as such, it is the only work now published.

Winding through the center of the village, and extending several miles beyond it on either side, is a shallow valley, in which are situated the

MINERAL SPRINGS,

the most celebrated in the world. There are in the immediate vicinity nearly thirty springs of acknowledged medicinal value. These thirty, which comprise the Saratoga Springs, are in the center of the crescent-shaped valley, the west horn of which is Ballston, and the east, Quaker Springs. The High Rock spring was the first discovered. Sir Wm. Johnson was carried to it by the Indians in 1767.

Most of the springs belong to the class known as carbonated, though some of them possess the properties of the sulphureted, the chalybeate and the saline. The mineral matter consists chiefly of chloride of sodium or common salt, carbonates of magnesia, lime, soda and lithia, and the sulphates of potassa, together with a small amount of other substances. The solvent power which holds all these solid substances in solution, and which gives them their agreeable taste, is the carbonic acid gas with which the water is so freely charged.

This free carbonic acid gas is probably formed by the decomposition of the carbonates which compose the rock. The water, impregnated with it, becomes a powerful solvent, and, passing through different strata, absorbs the various mineral substances which compose its solid constituents. Through faults and ordinary fractures in the earth's crust extending through several geological strata, these waters rise to the surface, forced up, it is supposed, by hydrostatic pressure and that of the gas.

Numerous have been the attempts to prepare artificial spring waters, but with little success. The most eminent chemists and scientific men now acknowledge its impracticability. There may be substances which the chemistry of the present day fails to discover, and the chemical laboratory of nature can only be imitated, never equaled.

We may analyze the acorn, but we cannot produce from the results obtained any thing more than a faint resemblance, which lacks its peculiar properties as well as its life principle. Artificial waters are dangerous, and do a *double* injustice, to the person who expects benefit from them, and to the natural waters.

Those who wish nature's remedies should obtain them direct from her laboratory.

Before giving a detailed account of the principal springs, we devote a few words to their

GENERAL PROPERTIES.

These are almost as various as the fountains from which the mineral waters flow. Cathartic, tonic, alterative and diuretic, and sulphur water, of varied shade and differing strength, are found in Saratoga. Each spring has its own peculiar virtues that adapt it to certain forms of disease. Hence, it follows that mineral waters should not be drank promiscuously, but under the direction of a competent physician, who thoroughly understands the composition and peculiarities of each, if the utmost benefit would be obtained. Many imagine that if the waters do no good they certainly cannot do harm. A mistake this, and one which may result in serious injury.

Whatever claims the owners of some of the springs may advance, it should be known that all the cathartic waters are liable to do more injury than good in Consumption and many diseases of the lungs.

Many of the mineral springs of the old world are under the charge of superintendents appointed by law, and invalids are not permitted to use the waters without directions from a physician. What wonder, then, if many who come here with a vague idea of drinking the waters, and who select simply the spring which happens to be the most popular, should go away having experienced little benefit. Persons in good health, however, find the waters a pleasant and invigorating beverage, and, when taken in proper quantities, uninjurious. General directions for drinking the waters are given elsewhere, and, under the description of the different springs, may be found a statement of their particular properties.

There is no doubt of their power to promote evacuations of effete accumulations from the kidneys, skin and bowels.

Prof. J. W. Draper, the eminent physiologist, in speaking of the springs, says: "They restore suppressed, and correct vitiated secretions, and so renovate health, and are also the means of introducing many medicines into the system in a state of minute subdivision, in which they exert a powerful alterative and curative action."

THE CRYSTAL SPRING

in Park Place, Broadway, opposite Congress Park. C. R. Brown, Proprietor.

This spring was discovered and tubed in 1870, since which time it has become widely known. The analysis and properties are well set forth on page 45.

EUREKA SPRING,

on Spring Avenue, about a mile and a half above the village. Eureka Spring Co., Proprietors; A. R. Dyett, President.

The scenery in the vicinity of the Spring is very romantic. The waters are of special service in dyspepsia and kindred diseases, and are similar in properties and analysis to the other Saratoga springs. The waters are bottled, and may be found in New York and other cities. A few rods from the Eureka, the

WHITE SULPHUR SPRING,

of Saratoga, is situated. A large and commodious Bathing-house, with excellent and ample accommodations and superior facilities, affords Sulphur Water Baths.

THE SULPHUR SPRING IS SAID TO BE UNSURPASSED BY ANY IN THIS STATE. There is now no reason why invalids should resort to the other sulphur springs of the State, when they can find here sulphur water at least fully equal to any, while they enjoy the additional benefits of the varied mineral springs of Saratoga.

Frequent omnibuses convey passengers to and from the Spring for a moderate sum. A new avenue has been opened to the Spring.

THE EXCELSIOR SPRING,

A. R. Lawrence & Co., proprietors, is in a beautiful valley and amid most romantic scenery, about a mile north-east of the village.

It may be reached by passing up Spring avenue, which has just been graded and handsomely laid out, or by Lake avenue. The finest walk in Saratoga is through the woods to the Excelsior Spring. The water-works and Excelsior Lake, as well as the Mansion House, are in the immediate vicinity of the spring. The tubing is 56 feet deep.

This spring is a pleasant cathartic, and has also alterative, diuretic and tonic properties, and is moreover a very delightful beverage. Two or three glasses in the morning is the dose as a cathartic. As an alterative and diuretic, it should be taken in small quantities during the day. The highest medical authority of this country have indorsed this spring as possessing very valuable medicinal properties. It is one of the most delicious waters found in this mineral valley. While it is bottled extensively, it is also supplied in barrels, by a peculiar method, for selling on draught. Twelve feet below the surface of the spring, a block tin tube conveys the water into reservoirs or oak barrels, made gas-tight by a lining of block tin. These barrels are furnished with two tubes, one of which extends from the top nearly the entire length of the barrel, and the other, a short tube, is merely fitted into the top. Then, by filling the barrel through the long tube by hydrostatic pressure, the air is excluded and the gas is not allowed to escape.

When sold on draught, it is necessary simply to connect the long tube with the draught tube, and the short tube with an air pump, when the water can be forced out by the pressure of the air and will flow forth sparkling and delicious as at the spring.

The gentlemanly proprietors have illustrated circulars showing the process, and will explain to visitors their peculiar method with great courtesy.

In the immediate vicinity of the Excelsior are the

TEN SPRINGS,

undeveloped as yet, but possessing varied medicinal properties.

HATHORN SPRING,

on Spring street, just above Congress Hall. H. H. Hathorn, proprietor. This spring is the most central and conveniently located of any in Saratoga. It was discovered and tubed in 1868.

It is a cathartic water, similar to the Congress, but much superior. Dose from one to three glasses in the morning.

ANALYSIS BY PROF. C. F. CHANDLER, COLUMBIA COLLEGE SCHOOL OF MINES.

Chloride of Sodium...	509.968	grains.	Bicarbonate of Baryta	1.737	grains.
Chloride of Potassium	9.597	"	Bicarbonate of Iron..	1.128	"
Bromide of Sodium...	1.534	"	Sulphate of Potassa..	none.	
Iodide of Sodium.....	.198	"	Phosphate of Soda...	.006	"
Fluoride of Calcium..	a trace.		Biborate of Soda.....	a trace.	
Bicarbonate of Lithia.	11.447	"	Alumina...............	.131	"
Bicarbonate of Soda..	4.288	"	Silica..................	1.260	"
Bicarbonate Magnesia.	176.463	"	Organic matter.......	a trace.	
Bicarbonate of Lime..	170.646	"			
Bicarbonate Strontia..	a trace.		Total solid contents..	888.403	

Carbonic acid gas in one gallon, 375.747 inches. Density, 1.009.

HIGH ROCK CONGRESS SPRING

on Willow Walk, near the Seltzer and Star Springs. High Rock Congress Spring Co., Proprietors. Wm. Slocum, Superintendent.

The High Rock is the oldest and most famous spring in Saratoga. It was the Bethesda of the Indians, and by them regarded with the greatest reverence. For over a hundred years it has been used by white men, and it is more popular to-day than ever before. The rock which gives

HIGH ROCK IN 1867.

the spring its name is still regarded as one of the greatest curiosities of the world; and although remote from the large hotels, is visited annually by large numbers of people. Similar deposits of mineral matter, forming calcareous tufa which constitutes High Rock, have been found at the surfaces of other springs; but this is *the great specimen.* The following are the dimensions of the rock: Circumference, 24 feet, 4 inches; height, 3 feet, 6 inches; diameter of aperature, 4 inches—below the top, 1 foot; weight, about 8 tons.

The rock is a hollow cone or pyramid, whose walls are of nearly even thickness. Of the genuineness of this rock there can be no doubt. Thousands of years were necessary for its formation, which can be traced by the rings or circles of deposit marking each year.

The proprietors of the High Rock Spring have issued a very interesting pamphlet, containing a full account of the High Rock and a history of the mineral spring. We commend this work to those who wish a more complete account than we have room to give of this marvelous work of nature. The pamphlet may be obtained free of charge at the spring.

The recent tubing, which is about ten feet south of the mouth of the old spring, has greatly improved its quality, and *it now bottles free from sediment,* and preserves its refreshing taste and medicinal properties for years. It is a very superior tonic and cathartic, as well as alterative. It may be drank at any time during the day.

Three or four glasses before breakfast will produce a cathartic effect.

In 1868 a superb colonnade — a pavilion within a pavilion — was erected over the spring, at an expense of over $5,000. It is of Gothic architecture, surmounted by a mosque-like dome and an immense gilded eagle, making it indeed a most attractive pagoda.

GEYSER OR SPOUTING SPRING,

about a mile and a half below the village on the Ballston road and near the railroad.

This wonderful mineral fountain was discovered in February, 1870. There had been indications of mineral springs in this neighborhood for a long time. Messrs Vail and Seavy, the owners of the bolt factory beneath which the fountain was discovered, determined to bore for a spring. They were successful, and when they had reached a point 140 feet below the surface rock, they struck the mineral vein. The water immediately burst forth with vehemence, and the marvelous phenomenon of a spouting spring was established.

The orifice bored in the rock is 5½ inches in diameter and 140 feet deep, 80 feet in the strata of slate and 60 feet in the birdseye limestone. The water continues to spout incessantly to the height of about 25 feet.

The tubing is a block-tin pipe encased with iron, 85 feet in length and two inches in diameter. It is noticeable that when a portion of the stream is directed to the bottling room for bottling purposes the fountain spouts to an unusual height.

The temperature of the spring is 46 deg. Fahr. being only 14 deg. from the freezing point. The water, an analysis of which is given elsewhere, is the most strongly impregnated with mineral and medicinal substances of any spring in the world. As the water is drawn from the fountain it foams like soda water, from the great abundance of carbonic acid gas, which gives it a very agreeable taste. It is strongly cathartic, alterative and tonic; dose from one to two glasses. The waters are now being bottled, and are sold in all the leading cities of America and Europe.

The fact that the spring is located 140 feet beneath the solid rock renders it free from all impurities of surface waters.

In the immediate vicinity of the spring is a beautiful cascade, lake and ravine, a white sulphur spring and the Ellis Spring, all objects of interest.

The Geyser Spring is one of the greatest attractions of Saratoga, and no visitor should fail to see it and taste its sparkling water.

THE PAVILION SPRING.

Pavilion Spring Co., proprietors. S. W. Frost, Sec'y and Supt., in the valley, a few rods east of Broadway, between Lake avenue and Caroline street.

This spring, although discovered long before, was not tubed till 1839.

We copy the following account of the process of tubing: "A curb 22 feet square, made of logs locked together at the corners, was built about the spring. The excavation next followed, and as the earth was thrown out the curb was settled down. As the work proceeded the water was raised from the shaft by large pumps used day and night, and thus the excavation was made to a distance of forty feet, following throughout the direction of the rising bubbles of gas." Here they reached the hard-pan. As the gas seemed to come from the west, they cut a trench in that direction, sideways and downwards, for several feet. In this trench the tube, shaped like a shoe, was placed, and a perpendicular tube, reaching to the surface, was fitted to the upper end of the shoe. Thus the tubing was completed and the earth around it replaced.

In 1869 the spring was retubed, and by moving the tube

down ten feet to the solid rock, the mineral quality increased.

The location of the Pavilion Spring is central, being only a few steps from the business portion of the village and the various hotels. The water possesses a pungent taste, yet is pleasant and exhilarating. In general, the properties are cathartic, diuretic and tonic. It is particularly good in billious diseases, scrofula, rheumatism, etc.

The sulphate of potassa and the bicarbonate of lithia in large quantity are found only in this spring. The use of the waters increase the appetite and digestion. As a cathartic, from one to four glasses should be taken in the morning. The water was first bottled in 1840. The present company was formed in 1868, and since the Spring has been retubed, the waters are having a more extended sale.

A very elegant colonnade in the beautiful park surrounding it renders the spring attractive to visitors. Within a few feet of the Pavilion, and under the same colonnade, is the

UNITED STATES SPRING.

While excavating for the purpose of retubing the Pavilion spring, a new spring, flowing from the east, was discovered.

This has been tubed, its waters analyzed, and they are now presented to the public.

This water is more gentle in its action and more tonic in its effects. As a tonic, from a half to two tumblers several times during the day is necessary.

THE RED SPRING

is located on Spring avenue, at the junction of Geneva and Warren streets, a few rods above the Empire spring. John A. Carpenter & Co., proprietors.

This spring, though over a century old, and of acknowledged medicinal value, has not been properly appreciated until recently.

In 1867 it was retubed and renovated, and since that time, under the direction of its present enterprising proprietors, its popularity has been rapidly increasing and its properties better understood.

Since last season an elegant pavilion and a neat and tasteful bottling-house have been erected.

This Spring is widely different from any other in Saratoga, and possesses peculiar merits. In a general sense, its therapeutic effects are alterative, but it possesses a particular adaptation to inflamed mucous surfaces. In cutaneous diseases it has a high reputation. In many cases of chronic dyspepsia, it has been of the greatest service. Snuffed up the nostrils for nasal catarrh, it removes the inflammation from the mucous surface, as it does from the stomach or bowels when taken internally. Its general effect is to *tone up* the system, regulate the secretions and vitalize the blood, thereby creating a better appetite and better assimulation. It is claimed, by those who have tried it, to be a sure cure for salt rheum, etc.

Many persons are benefited by this water who cannot bear the more saline springs.

SELTZER SPRING.

"Saratoga Seltzer Spring Co.," proprietors. Perhaps no one of the springs attracts more visitors or gratifies the curious more than the Seltzer.

It is situated about 150 feet from the High Rock Congress spring, but, although in such close proximity thereto, its water is entirely different, thus illustrating the wonderful extent and capacity of nature's subterranean laboratory.

The owners of the Seltzer spring have an ingenious contrivance for exhibiting the flow of the water and its gas. It consists of a glass tube, three feet in height and fifteen inches in diameter, nicely adjusted to the mouth of the spring, through which the sweet, clear, sparkling water gushes in a steady volume, while, faster than the water, bubble up the glittering globules of pure carbonic acid gas.

The spring was discovered several years ago, but only recently was it tubed so as to be available. The tube extends down thirty-four feet to the surface of the foundation rock. The crevice in the rock through which the water issues is about twelve inches by five. The column of water above the rock is thirty-seven feet high. The flow of gas is abundant and constant, but every few minutes, as the watchful visitor will observe, there is a momentary ebullition of an extraordinary quantity which causes the water in the tube to boil over the rim. When the sunshine falls upon the fountain it presents a beautiful appearance.

This is the only Seltzer spring in this country. The character of the water is almost identical with that of the

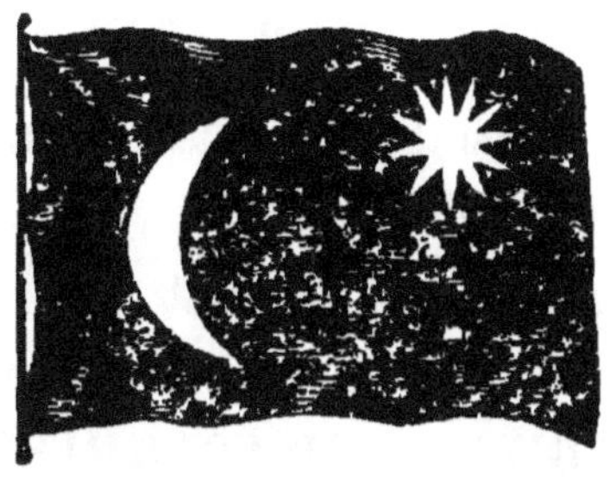

celebrated Nassau spring of Germany, which is justly esteemed so delicious by the natives of the "Fatherland." Our German citizens, with their usual sagacity, have discovered this fact, and the consumption of the water by them is daily on the increase.

The importance of this American Seltzer spring will be somewhat appreciated by the reader, when informed of the fact that nearly two millions of stone jugs, holding one quart each, of the Nassau Seltzer are annually exported from Germany.

The water of this spring is very pleasant to the taste, being slightly acidulous and saline, but much milder than that of the other Saratoga springs. It is an agreeable and wholesome beverage. When mixed with still wines, etc., it adds the peculiar flavor only to be derived from a pure, natural Seltzer. It enlivens them and gives them the character of sparkling wines.

Its use as a refreshing beverage and for its remedial qualities is already widely extended, and its popularity rapidly on the increase.

Saratoga possesses numerous objects of interest for the German population, surpassing even the famous Spas of Europe, and the discovery of the Seltzer will doubtless attract large numbers of this intelligent and genial people.

The analysis of both the Saratoga and the German Seltzer springs is given on page 44.

THE STAR SPRING,

on Willow Walk, near the termination of Circular street. Star Spring Company, proprietors; A. Putnam, Jr., Supt. Reached from Front street by steps.

The waters of this spring have been used for a long time, and have a high reputation. By the recent retubing their mineral quality has been increased and rendered purer. The water is a pleasant beverage, differing somewhat in taste from the other springs. By recent inventions of the superintendent, Mr. Putnam, the water is now presented to the public in a new way, having many advantages over the old method of bottling. Iron casks are lined with porcelain, and are provided with Mr. Putnam's patent faucet, which absolutely prevents the escape of gas while drawing the water, or at any time. The faucet consists of several air chambers, closely fitted together, with valves, and connecting with a block-tin tube, reaching to the top of the cask. By these inventions the proprietor feels confident that even champagne might be barreled, so difficult or impossible is it for the gas to escape. Among other advantages of this novel method of putting up water, is its cheapness, and the privilege of being able to obtain a drink of Saratoga water at a moment's notice. The water is also bottled in the usual way for those who prefer. In 1870 the Star Company erected the handsome structure in which their casks and bottles are now filled.

The office is very elegant, and Mr. Wright, their book-keeper, has adorned it with a large variety of beautiful plants and flowers.

COLUMBIAN SPRING,

in Congress park, near the Congress spring. This is a chalybeate or iron water; it is a strong tonic, and when taken before breakfast, or in too great quantity, is apt to cause a peculiar headache. It is very different from most of the other springs, and should be used with care. Only from a half to one glass should be taken at a time. It also has a diuretic action, and has been used extensively for that purpose.

CONGRESS SPRING,

in Congress park, on Congress street. This spring is famous as one of the oldest springs of Saratoga. It is a cathartic water. Dose, from three to seven glasses before breakfast.

HAMILTON SPRING,

on Spring street, corner of Putnam, in the rear of Congress Hall, and a short distance from Hathorn spring. Its principal action is diuretic, and, in large doses, cathartic. The mineral ingredients are the same as those of the other springs, but, owing to the peculiar combination, the medicinal effects are widely different. It has been found of great service in kidney complaints. From one to three glasses during the day is the usual dose. It should be used under the prescription of a physician, and warm drinks should not be taken immediately after. It is not bottled.

PUTNAM SPRING,

on Phila street, near Broadway. Used chiefly for bathing purposes. It is a tonic or chalybeate, and, as this goes to press, is being re-tubed.

EMPIRE SPRING

a few rods above the Star spring, and similar to it, but containing a less quantity of mineral constituents.

SARATOGA "A" SPRING

was located a few rods from the Red spring. The bottling-house was burned down in 1867, and the water is no longer bottled or used.

WASHINGTON SPRING,

in the grounds of the Clarendon Hotel, South Broadway, sometimes called the "Champagne spring," on account of its sparkling properties. This is one of the pleasantest waters in Saratoga. It is a delicious beverage as well as a superior tonic. The grounds in the immediate vicinity are very picturesque, and are thronged by the most fashionable. In the evening, the grounds are lighted by gas, and large numbers visit the spring. It was first tubed in 1806, before any other in this mineral valley. We learn that in 1828 "the waters of this fountain were seldom drank on account of its remote situation, but were resorted to by the indigent for the purpose of external application, and were found to be of eminent service when applied to old, ill-conditioned ulcers, and obstinate eruptions of the skin."*

At the present day it is one of the most popular springs. It was never properly tubed till 1858–9, when the tubing was accomplished with the greatest difficulty. The water is bottled to some extent. The dose is from one to two glasses. It should be used for a long time to secure the full benefit.

In the same grounds, and within one or two rods, is the LELAND SPRING, which at the present writing has not been developed.

ELLIS SPRING

on the Ballston road near the Geyser. This is the only spring which flows in a horizontal direction, issuing from the hillside and flowing down the valley. It is very similar to the Columbian in its properties. It has been long known, but is used very little. It is a pleasant beverage.

Mineral water has been found in other localities, but at present the above is a **complete list** of the SARATOGA MINERAL SPRINGS.

We have endeavored to represent them fairly, and in our description of them have stated nothing that we have not had ample reason to believe.

DIRECTIONS FOR DRINKING THE WATERS.

It is impossible to give *complete and invariable* directions for drinking any of the waters.

---

* An analysis of the mineral waters of Saratoga and Ballston, by Dr. J. H. Steel, 1828.

The experience and necessities of each individual can alone determine many things in regard to their use.

It is advisable to consult some experienced resident physician who understands the properties of all of the springs *and yet has no immediate interest in either of them.*

The CATHARTIC waters, as a cathartic, should be taken only before breakfast in the morning, and possibly before retiring at night, because in the morning the body, refreshed by sleep, is best prepared for the water, and the stomach is empty. The water should be drank slowly, and, if more than one glass is taken, it should be after a suitable interval. Before eating, the sipping of a little tea or coffee will make the waters more efficacious.

None of the cathartic waters should be drank immediately before, during or within two hours after meals, as they are then liable to disturb digestion and prevent nutrition.

As an ALTERATIVE, the waters should be drank in small quantities at various intervals during the day. As their alterative effect is from the absorption of the water, the quantity taken should be small.

The chalybeate or TONIC waters are liable to cause headache when taken before breakfast. They may be used with benefit before or after dinner and tea. Only from a half to one glass should be taken at a time.

The DIURETIC waters should be drank before meals, and at night, and should not be followed by warm drinks.

The enormous quantities of water which some persons imbibe at the popular springs is perfectly shocking, and can only be injurious. It is no uncommon occurrence to see persons drink from five to ten glasses of Congress or Hathorn water with scarcely any interval, and the writer has heard of a lady who swallowed within a few minutes fourteen glasses of one of the springs. It is to be presumed that her thirst was satisfied, as no further account of her has been given.

Those who are taking a course of mineral water will usually find their appetite increased thereby.

An abundance of vegetables should be avoided, and only those which are perfectly fresh should be used.

Frequent bathing in mineral water and otherwise will be found beneficial.

BOTTLING OF THE WATERS.

The first attempt to extend the benefits of the spring water beyond the limits of Saratoga was made by Gideon Putnam. He secured two large potash kettles for evapo rating the mineral water, and sold in packages, quite extensively, the salts which were precipitated. It was not long, however, before it was discovered that spring water could not be reproduced by dissolving these salts. About the year 1826 the bottling of the water was first commenced, and, since that time, has become a very flourishing and extensive business. The work of bottling at the principal springs is kept up during the year, except for a few weeks of the fashionable season.

The present mode, in its various processes, requires considerable care and time before the cases of water are shipped to the market. Particular attention is paid to the cleansing of the bottles. The finest of corks are imported, and are first soaked in hot water, till they become perfectly compressible. The spring water is pumped into the bottling house through block-tin pipes, and from a small receiver the bottles are filled. The corks are then driven in by machinery and the bottles packed away in bins of several hundred dozen.

Here they are allowed to remain four or five days, to test the strength of the bottles and to ascertain if any of the corks are leaky.

The expansion of the gas is so great that it requires strong bottles to retain it. Where imperfections exist, as they frequently do, the bottles will burst, sometimes with a loud report.

Having been thouroughly tested, the corks of the bottles are secured by a copper wire and packed in the cases with great care. When the case is filled, the packer walks on the bottles, to again test their strength and to prevent any liability of breakage after the boxes leave the establishment. With all these precautions, it is no wonder that the cases of spring water, however roughly handled, always reach their destination perfectly secure, and without the escape of the carbonic acid gas.

The amount of the water which is bottled in this manner at some of the springs amounts to two hundred dozen bottles a day.

To supply the bottles for this immense business, a large

GLASS FACTORY

has been erected south of the village and near the railroad, and is well worth a visit.

HOTELS.

Saratoga has the largest and most extensive in the world. There are in all from thirty to forty, and in addition to them numerous public and private boarding-houses accomodate a large number of guests. We have room to notice only the largest and best.

The gem of Saratoga, and one the finest, if not *the finest*, hotel in this country is

CONGRESS HALL.

Extending from Spring to Congress street, with a front on Broadway of 416 feet, and reaching with its two mammoth wings 300 feet back, it is architecturally a perfect beauty. The rooms are large and elegant. The halls are 10 feet wide, and broad, commodious stairways, with the finest elevator in the country render every portion readily accessible. A front piazza, 20 feet wide and 240 feet in length, with numerous others within the grounds, and a promenade on the top of the hotel affording a charming view, contribute to render the house attractive. The dining halls, parlors, etc., are superb and ample, and every thing about the house is on a scale of unequaled magnificence and grandeur.

The proprietors have endeavored to incorporate into this hotel every thing that can aford comfort and pleasure, at whatever expense.

The cut of Congress Hall, on the cover, will give some idea of its *outlines*, but fails to do it justice. It must be

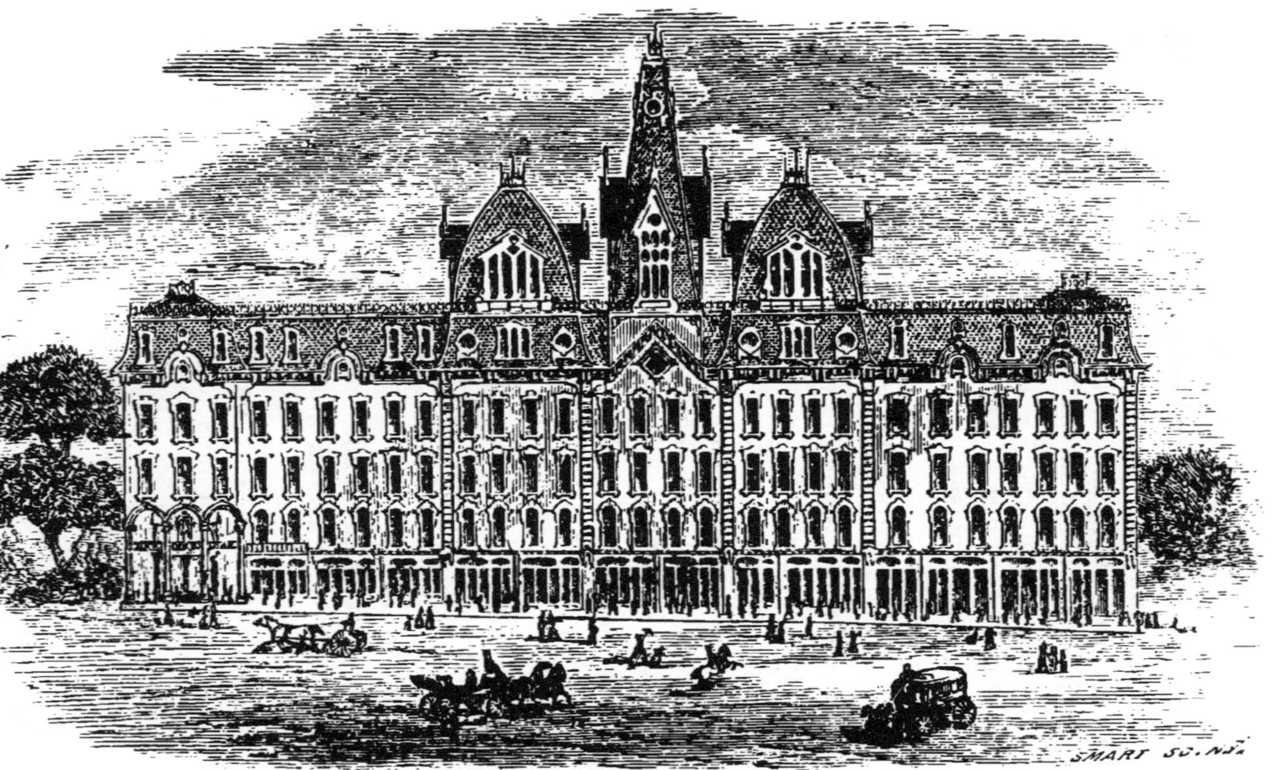

PARK PLACE HOTEL, Broadway, C. R. BROWN, Proprietor.

seen to be appreciated, and when seen commands the unqualified admiration of the beholder.

UNION HALL.

This mammoth concern is located on Broadway, opposite Congress Hall. It has a front on Broadway of 450 feet, and attractive grounds in the rear. The public office of this house is said to be the finest hotel office in the world. It is 50 by 70 feet, and is elegantly fitted up with white and colored marbles. A series of colonnades rise from the center of the office to the dome. This hotel accommodates more guests than any other, but one, in the world.

Warren Leland is the present manager.

THE CLARENDON

is patronized by a very cultivated and select class of guests. Its location is very picturesque; and within its inclosure, surrounded by magnificent pines and covered with a superb pagoda, is the celebrated Washington spring.

The Leland spring, named in honor of the affable proprietor of the hotel, is also within the grounds.

A few steps above the new town hall, on Broadway, in a quiet and yet central location, is the

WAVERLY HOUSE,

of which Mr. Wm. C. Jones is proprietor. Last year the house was newly furnished throughout, and just before the opening of the present season outside and inside have been rendered even more attractive by the painter's brush, while various other improvements have been made.

The rooms of this hotel are very large and airy. A double piazza, 340 feet in length, entirely surrounds the house, affording a splendid promenade and a delightful place to while away a summer afternoon. The many brilliant equipages and dashing turnouts, which render Broadway so attractive, are here seen in their glory. The High Rock, Empire, Star and Red springs are only a few steps from the house.

The proprietor designs to afford the greatest comfort and and at reasonable rates.

THE EVERETT HOUSE,

on South Broadway, a few steps beyond the Clarendon, is well patronized by a wealthy and cultivated class of guests. A very pleasant piazza surrounding the front of the house, and a pretty lawn and cottage in the grounds, are attractive features of this summer hotel. The house has a home-like appearance and a delightful location.

THE CONTINENTAL HOTEL,

on Washington street, is well kept, and enjoys a high reputation. Its rooms are very large and pleasant. It is well represented in the cut, and is really one of the best hotels of Saratoga.

THE CRESCENT HOTEL,

under the management of Dr. R. Hamilton, is an excellent place to stop. Although a medical institute is connected with it, it is entirely free from any objections that may be supposed to pertain to such, but is rendered more desirable thereby.

TEMPLE GROVE.

This House will be open for Boarders from the 17th of June to the 5th of September.

The Rooms are large and pleasant. The Grounds are ample and well shaded.

The Terms for Board will be from $18 to $25 per week, according to time, accommodations, rooms, etc. Transient Board $3.50 per day. A discount of 10 per cent will be made to all clergymen actually engaged in the gospel ministry.

Families taken at special rates.

The Omnibus for TEMPLE GROVE will be at the Station to meet all Trains.

HENRY M. DOWD,

PROPRIETOR.

There are few places more lovely or possessing more attractions for those who wish retirement and rest, than the surroundings of the

MANSION HOUSE,

near the Excelsior, Eureka and White Sulphur springs and Excelsior Lake. Mrs. E. G. Chipman, who has recently become the proprietress, will render it a delightful home.

BOARDING-HOUSES

abound in all parts of the village. Some are very large and commodious, and others private and home-like. A list of the largest and best, so far as we have been able to ascertain, is inserted elsewhere.

The Vermont House, on Grove, corner Front street, is furnished in excellent style and is neat and tidy. The parlors and dining rooms would do credit to many of the hotels in point of finish. It is a well-kept boarding-house.

The Huestis House, the Pitney House and Washington Hall are among the largest. Many people prefer these boarding-houses to the large hotels.

ANALYSIS OF THE Saratoga Seltzer Water

By C. F. CHANDLER, Ph. D.

In one gallon of 231 cubic inches are contained—

	SARATOGA SELTZER. (C. F. Chandler.)		GERMAN SELTZER. (Kastner.)	
Chloride of Sodium,	134.291	grains.	132.673	grains
Chloride of Potassium,	1.335	"	0.469	"
Bromide of Sodium,	0.630	"	0.001	"
Iodide of Sodium,	0.031	"		
Fluoride of Calcium,	trace.		0.012	"
Bicarbonate of Lithia,	0.899	"	.005	"
Bicarbonate of Soda,	29.428	"	74.773	"
Bicarbonate of Magnesia,	40.339	"	22.354	"
Bicarbonate of Lime,	89.869	"	22.937	"
Bicarbonate of Strontia,	trace.		0.083	"
Bicarbonate of Baryta,	trace.			
Bicarbonate of Iron,	1.703	"	0.919	"
Bicarbonate of Manganese,			0.027	"
Sulphate of Potassa,	0.557	"	2.217	"
Biborate of Soda,	trace.			
Phosphate of Soda,	trace.		2.132	"
Alumina,	0.374	"	trace.	
Silica,	2.561	"	1.905	"
TOTAL,	302.017	grains.	260.507	grains.
Carbonic Acid Gas,	324.08	cu. in.	228.73	cu. in.

Temperature of Water at Spring, Saratoga, 50° Fah.

THE SARATOGA WATER IS UNSURPASSED FOR MIXTURE WITH RED AND WHITE WINES.

Orders for the Water received by

FREDERICK ROWLEY, Superintendent, SARATOGA SPRINGS, N. Y.,

Or by EBERT & GROSVENOR, Sole Agents, Depot of the Company, 125 HUDSON STREET, NEW YORK CITY.

Small Bottles per Doz. $2. Large Bottles per Doz. $3.

ALSO SOLD IN TANKS HOLDING 10 AND 20 GALLONS.

TEMPLE GROVE SEMINARY.

This Institution is beautifully situated in a grove in the eastern part of the village, on what was formerly called Temple Hill, hence the name. The grounds occupy the whole square on Spring street, between Circular and Regent streets.

All the noted springs of Saratoga are within a few minutes walk of the Seminary, while Congress Park is but one block distant. The Institution is under the efficient management of Charles F. Dowd, A. M., a graduate of Yale College, and it affords the best advantages for a complete and solid education.

The "Regular Graduating Course" occupies a period of four years, and embraces the principal studies pursued in our best colleges for young men, while much liberty is allowed to "optional studies," which supply the more modern and artistic accomplishments. Every facility for improvement which libraries and apparatus can afford is found at this institution ; and the religious and moral culture of the students is conscientiously cared for in a liberal and faithful Christian spirit.

Among the patrons of the Seminary are some of the best families of the leading cities of the country. These superior advantages are afforded at very reasonable charges. The endowment is found in the fact that during the long vacation of the summer months, from June to September, the building is opened as a summer resort. At this time its spacious and well furnished rooms, and well supplied table, under the efficient direction of Henry M. Dowd, dispense to its select patrons the greatest comforts and luxuries of the very first-class hotels. Its omnibus runs to the depot to meet all trains. The delightful grove and grounds, a few steps removed from the bustle and confusion of the great hotels, and its accessibility to all the springs in Saratoga, renders the Seminary particularly desirable to lovers of health and comfort.

SARATOGA AS A HEALTH RESORT.

The world-wide fame of Saratoga as a fashionable watering place is not greater than its reputation as a health resort. Without doubt, it possesses greater advantages for the recovery of health than any other place in America, if not in the world. These advantages are not merely its wonderful healing waters, for which it is so justly celebrated. The climate of Saratoga is peculiarly salubrious. On the north and west the Kayaderosseras mountain affords its protection and shelter, and the Green mountain range on the east, with the Catskills on the south, combine to shield the village from raw winds and drifting storms. Adorned with the most beautiful groves of pine and fir, the atmosphere is said to resemble that of Minnesota.

The village is sufficiently rural for quiet and retirement, while it affords many advantages to be found only in large cities.

The combination of these circumstances point to Saratoga as the great physical Mecca. Hither come from near and far hundreds of pilgrims, worn out by professional duties or the activities of business life, and sufferers from the various chronic diseases that flesh is heir to.

Since the number of health-seekers is so great, it is

natural that particular accomodations should be made for them. To supply this want, several large and flourishing

HEALTH INSTITUTIONS

have arisen. Their success has been unqualified. The advantages afforded are not merely a change of climate and habits, but embrace facilities and remedial appliances unavailable in general practice.

The institutions of Saratoga have a wide reputation. As no Guide to the place would be complete, without an account of them, we publish here some of the features of the most celebrated.

THE REMEDIAL INSTITUTE of Drs. S. S. & S. E. Strong is located on Circular, between Spring and Phila streets, and just above Temple Grove. It is probably surpassed by no institution in this country or Europe, in the elegance of its appointments and the completeness of its appliances. The house will accomodate about two hundred guests. Its patrons are from the most cultivated Christian people of the land. Among the large number of clergymen who make this their summer home is the distinguished Dr. Cuyler, who has made his annual visits to Saratoga for over twenty successive summers.

The institute is finished in the very best taste and heated by steam, while the bath rooms are exceedingly elegant, and are *one of the chief attractions of Saratoga*.

Among the special appliances which are used in the treatment of invalids, is the Equalizer or vacuum treatment, electro-thermal baths, Swedish movement cure, vibrator, Russian bath, sulphur air bath, oxygen gas, Turkish and every other form of bath.

A very neat pamphlet describing these appliances and their *modus operandi* has been issued by the doctors, who are graduates of the medical department of New York University, and have attained eminent rank in their profession. As a *summer home* this house fully meets the wants of those desiring first-class accomodations, and its remedial character does not diminish its attractions.

DR. HAMILTON'S MEDICAL INSTITUTE is located on Broadway, corner Congress street, and opposite Congress Park.

This institution is a delightful home. In addition to the various remedial appliances which contribute to the recovery of invalids, including the celebrated Swedish movement cure, electro-chemical baths, oxygenized air bath rooms, health lift, numerous means of healthful recreation are also provided. Daily devotions and frequent social and religious meetings are characteristic features of the house. Comfort and pleasure are afforded at reasonable prices. During the warm season the house is opened to the public, and affords first-class accommodations to the large numbers of cultivated people who make it their summer home.

The proprietor, Dr. Hamilton, has had a large practice and is widely known throughout the country.

DRS. BEDORTHA'S WATER CURE has a pleasant location on Broadway, opposite Congress spring and Park. This is the oldest medical institution in Saratoga, and, during the long time since its establishment, it has made many friends. It has been patronized by large numbers from all parts of the country, and has a wide-spread name.

The Invalids' Guide, by Dr. N. Bedortha, contains an account of the mode of treatment and remedies used in the institution.

In addition to these medical institutions, numerous physicians devote special attention to the visiting population and to the medicinal use of the waters.

DRIVES AND WALKS.

The most fashionable drive is the new Boulevard to the Lake. This drive is four miles in length, with a row of trees on each side and one in the middle. Carriages pass down on one side and return on the other. For a long time it has been the principal drive in Saratoga, but until recently there have been few attractions besides the gay and brilliant procession of carriages with their fair occupants and superb horses. Since last season immense sums of money have been expended on the avenues and roads in the vicinity of Saratoga, and this new boulevard is now a very magnificent drive, although not completed as yet. Near the outlet of the lake, on a bluff fifty feet above the surface of the water, is Moon's Lake House, one of the features of Saratoga. The grounds around the house are attractive, and command a fine view of the lake. The hobby of the Lake House is Fried Potatoes, and these they serve in good style. They are sold in papers like confectionery.

CHAPMAN'S HILL, a mile beyond the Lake House, is one hundred and eighty feet above the level of the lake. A charming view is obtained from the hill, but not as fine as is afforded from

WAGMAN'S HILL, three miles beyond, and sixty feet higher.

HAGERTY HILL, six miles north of the village, toward Luzerne, brings to view a fine landscape.

BEMIS' HEIGHTS, the scene of the famous engagement between Burgoyne and General Gates, is about fifteen miles distant, in Stillwater, and is visited by large numbers of people.

But the most extended view and the boldest landscape may be seen from WARING HILL, on the Mount Pleasant road, and about fifteen miles from Saratoga Springs.

Saratoga, Ballston, Schenectady, Waterford, Mechanicsville, Schuylerville, Saratoga lake, Round lake, etc., etc., by the aid of a glass, can all be discerned from this hill. There are other and shorter drives in Saratoga which are very attractive. Spring avenue, leading to the Excelsior and Sulphur springs, and round by Lake avenue, is very pleasant. The road to Ballston and the Geyser spring has recently been improved.

The entire length of Broadway is a magnificent drive,

About a mile above Congress Hall the half-mile track and handsome grounds of Glen Mitchel are located.

By far the most beautiful walk in Saratoga is the WALK THROUGH THE GROVE TO THE EXCELSIOR SPRING. Carriages and omnibuses may be taken as far as the grove. A pleasant hour may be spent in the woods, after a stroll through which, the delicious water of the Excelsior spring will be refreshing indeed.

Congress Park is a lovely place and a great resort. There are many other walks in almost every direction which the pedestrian will find interesting.

AMUSEMENTS.

Of these the chief is flirting and dancing. Every afternoon the various bands at the large hotels discourse delicious music. The various drives, croquet, and a visit to the circular railway and Indian encampment, are enjoyed by many. During race week the races are the all-absorbing theme. The evening finds a brillant party in the various ball-rooms, while at the more retired hotels and boarding-houses, charades and tableaux give opportunity for the display of wit and beauty. The streets are thronged with a gay and brilliant multitude, engaged in riding, driving or walking, each enjoying to the utmost a fascinating kind of busy idleness. The attractions of Saratoga society are famous.

Those who are not matrimonially inclined should know that during their sojourn at the Spa, they are surrounded by dangers on every hand. Cupid for many years has made Saratoga his summer home.

GAMBLING AND OTHER VICES.

A few steps from Congress spring, and directly opposite the park, stands the club-house or gambling establishment of John Morrissey.

Few are the journals of city or country, in even the remote sections of our land, that have not contained some account or allusion to Mr. Morrissey's establishment.

It has become one of the first objects to which the attention of visitors is attracted.

A very exaggerated idea of its magnificence has been excited by so much talk and the glowing accounts of *penny-a-liners.*

For instance, we are told that one of the "very finest" oil paintings in the country adorned its walls, but when we came to investigate we learned that the expense of this "magnificent work of art" amounted to about $3,500. We concluded that either Mr. M. was exceedingly shrewd in purchasing or else the finest paintings were at a discount.

The building is very substantial, and is well furnished. That its finish and furnishings are superior or equal to the first class residences of our cities is by no means true.

During the past winter a large addition has been made to it, the main object of which, it is said, is for the selling of pools for the races. This is by far the finest part of the building.

The case of the Y. M. C. A. *v.* Morrissey remains yet undecided, but that association closed three other establishments for the same purpose. During the winter and spring such efforts have been made by the leading citizens of Saratoga to restrain, within proper bounds, the vices and crimes incident to any fashionable resort, that it may be hoped that Saratoga will become the most moral, as it is now the most celebrated, watering-place in the world. Large numbers of the most cultivated, as well as the most wealthy, people are among the summer residents of Saratoga, and a majority of its citizens will sustain this action for the suppression of open vice.

THE SARATOGA MARBLE WORKS.

The tourist, interested in science, or fond of the beautiful, will find a new attraction in Saratoga this year, in the steam mills and magnificent marbles of The Adirondack Verd-Antique Marble Co. The workshops where the marble receives its shape are located in this village, near the freight depot. The quarries are situated in the town of Thurman, Warren county, some seven miles north-west of Thurman station, on the Adirondack railroad.

This peculiar rock embraces an area of about seventy-five acres, lying in ridges of some forty to sixty feet above the water level, and surrounded by the common gneissoid granite of that region. The depth of the bed, judging from geological indications, is not less than four hundred feet.

The marble consists of lime, magnesia and silex in a metamorphic condition. It is variously colored, combining the black and green of the Lapland, and the light and dark mottled greens of the Etruscan and Franconian verdantiques, with an almost endless variety of shadings and blendings of coloring.

The marble occupies a portion of a basin-shaped valley surrounded by hills, some of them rising to the height of fifteen hundred feet.

Unlike other varieties of the ornamental marbles, this admits of being worked in very thin slabs without cementation, as the magnesia forms the vinculum or paste by which the grains or particles of which it is composed are held together, and performs the same office as magnesia does in forming hydraulic lime of the common carbonates. This property enables it to be cut sharper, to sustain pressure, and to withstand the action of the weather in a manner very much superior to any of the white marbles.

This deposit, whose geological position is in the upper group or division of the Laurentian series of rocks, has been considered azoic, and deposited long prior to the appearance of any organized existence on the earth, but more acute investigation has revealed the fact that it is almost entirely made up of organic remains, — the EOZOON CANADENSE, THE OLDEST KNOWN FOSSIL ON THE GLOBE. The Eozoon Canadense was a foraminiferous creature of microscopic dimensions, which lived in communities and built up its stony receptacles in the ocean, in a manner analogous to the corals of the present time. In the fossil remains muriatic acid develops the structure in a bautiful manner. Scattered through the marble are large patches of transparent noble serpentine, some of which are extremely beautiful, resembling moss agate.

Specimens of this marble, highly polished, are on exhibition at the office on Broadway, and at the workshop. Scientific men will doubtless speedily avail themselves of this opportunity to procure for their center tables a marble top composed of the remains of the earliest form of existence known.

SARATOGA AS A PLACE OF RESIDENCE.

Saratoga has been so modest that its many advantages as a place of residence are often overlooked. That it possesses not a few unusual and delightful attractions, while it is not behind other places of its size in scarcely any respect, must be acknowledged. Not alone the constant use of its spring waters, but its dry and bracing climate, its magnificent groves and finely shaded streets, these and numerous other favorable circumstances contribute to make Saratoga unsurpassed as a permanent home. At one portion of the year the most distinguished, cultivated and wealthy of our own country are gathered here, and sight seeing can be done at home and on our own doorsteps. The many blessings which follow in the train of wealth and culture are found here. Travelers from other climes who visit our country seldom return until they have drank from these celebrated fountains, and enjoyed the comforts of these mammoth hotels. An opportunity is afforded in the various pulpits of the village to listen to the most eloquent preachers of the day.

The home society of Saratoga is very pleasant, and uncorrupted by the flash and glitter of the summer carnival.

Notwithstanding all these benefits, which the resident population enjoy, the expense of living is moderate, and

THE RED SPRING AND BOTTLING HOUSE,
SPRING AVENUE.

certainly below other and less celebrated watering places. That these advantages are becoming appreciated is evinced by the numerous and costly dwellings that are being erected on almost every street.

The average rise in real estate has been about ten per cent per annum for several years, and it may be confidently hoped that this beautiful place, possessing such peculiar attractions, will become the center of a large population.

Educational institutions and manufacturing interests should flourish here. Tasteful cottages for summer residents are needed.

The present population is about 9,000. For information in regard to real estate and permanent or transient homes in Saratoga, our readers are referred to Messrs. Wm. M Searing & Son, Real Estate Agents, Ainsworth's place, Broadway.

LIST OF HOTELS AND PRINCIPAL BOARDING HOUSES.

Albemarle Hotel, Broadway.
Albion House, Front street.
American Hotel, Broadway, Bennett & McCaffrey.
Broadway Hall, Broadway, S. P. Briggs.
Broadway House, Broadway, J. Howland.
Cedar Bluff Hotel, Lake, H. U. Myers.
Circular Street House, Circular street, L. R. Simons.
Clarendon Hotel, Broadway, C. E. Leland.
Columbian Hotel, Broadway, P. S. Waugh.

Commercial Hotel, Church street, corner Matilda, S. W. Smith & Co.

Congress Hall, Broadway, H. H. Hathorn & Co.

Continental Hotel, Washington street, M. M. Smalley.

Cottage Home, Miss L. Burbanck.

Crescent Hotel, Broadway, corner Congress street, R. Hamilton.

Everett House, South Broadway, B. V. Frazier.

Empire Hotel, Front street, C. H. Kendall.

Glen Mitchel, Broadway, C. Weeks Mitchel.

Grand Union Hotel, Broadway, Leland.

Holden House, Broadway, W. J. Riggs.

Hotel Germania, Broadway, G. Schmidt.

Green Mountain House, Washington street, Chaffee & Wooster.

Huestis House, 34 Broadway, J. L. Huestis.

Lake House, Lake, C. B. Moon.

Lake Side House, Lake, C. B. Moon, Jr.

Manor House, South Broadway.

Mansion House, Spring avenue, near Excelsior spring, Mrs. E. G. Chipman.

Marvin House, Broadway, A. & D. Snyder.

Merchants Hotel, Caroline street, corner Henry, G. H. Burrows.

Mount Pleasant House, Broadway, C. H. Teft.

Osborn House, Front, corner Van Dam, Geo. F. White.

Pitney House, Congress street, J. Pitney.

Park Place Hotel, Broadway, C. R. Brown.

Pavilion Hotel, Division street, Eldridge & Co.

Summer Resort, Franklin street.

Temple Grove, Circular street, H. M. Dowd.

Vermont House, Grove street, corner Front, B. V. Dyer.

Waverly House, Broadway, Wm. C. Jones.

Western Hotel, Church street, corner Lawrence, French & Co.

Wilbur House, Washington street.

St. James Hotel, Congress street, Van Vleck.

WHERE TO TRADE IN SARATOGA.

For the convenience of visitors we publish below a notice of some of the best business houses. We have admitted no one in whom we have not confidence, and have said nothing in regard to them that we do not *fully indorse.*

BOOKS, STATIONERY, PERIODICALS, ETC.

Mr. E. R. Stevens, Jr., first door above Congress Hall, Broadway, keeps a good assortment, is polite and attentive to his customers, and has the latest issues. Music, as soon as published, may be found at his bookstore.

MEDICINES, TOILET ARTICLES, PERFUMERY, ETC.

F. T. Hill & Co., 162 Broadway, opposite the Marvin House. By personal experience we have found this house reliable, accurate and expeditious in pharmacy. They keep the best, and at reasonable prices.

DRY GOODS, MILLINERY, FANCY NOTIONS, ETC.

J. H. Carpenter & Co., Broadway, is a desirable place to trade. Those who wish for superior goods, at reasonable prices, will do well to give them a call.

BOOTS, SHOES AND RUBBERS

of the best style are kept by J. L. Lucas, 102 Broadway. A large assortment is kept constantly. Mr. Lucas is also the discoverer and manufacturer of Lucas' Russian Leather Preservative and Waterproof Dressing for boots and shoes.

HATS, CAPS, ETC.

Vibbard, the fashionable hatter, Ainsworth place, Broadway, has the best store, the largest assortment, and the most elegant styles in Saratoga.

DR. C. H. RICH, DENTIST,

Phila street opposite the Post-Office. Dr. Rich is a perfect gentleman as well as a *very superior dentist.*

CONFECTIONERY, ICE CREAM, SODA, ETC.

Scidmore & Van Deusen, 142 Broadway, have constantly on hand a large variety of the very best of Maillard's confectionary. They also have ice cream, soda water, etc.

BOARDING STABLE AND LIVERY.

Dexter's on Division street near the railroad station. Among the large number of liveries, Dexter's is one of the largest and best. His carriages and horses are first-class and his coachmen accommodating and civil. Mr. Dexter has also a first-class boarding stable, entirely distinct from the livery. The terms are reasonable. Should Mr. Bonner visit Saratoga this summer he will probably patronize Dexter.

LANDSCAPE VIEWS.

The most beautiful and artistic views, stereoscopic and cabinet, of Saratoga, Lake George, etc., with which we are acquainted, are made by Mr. S. R. Stoddard, who is also a portrait painter of acknowledged talent.

Very few visit these great watering places without wishing to take home with them some mementoes of their surroundings, and the want is supplied in Mr. Stoddard's views, embracing as they do many scenes of great beauty as well as interest, and making many of them what they were designed to be, really "*studies for artists.*"

TONSORIAL.

J. R. Wood & Waters, under Crescent Hotel, corner Congress street and Broadway, lather and shave in a superior manner. They are first-class barbers. Their rooms are neat and cosy, and have connected with them a bathing establishment for warm and cold baths.

Mr. Wood has gained an excellent patronage and many friends by his successful management while under the American. *Next, gentlemen.*

CRYSTAL SPRING,

PARK PLACE, BROADWAY.

C. R. BROWN, - - - Proprietor.

ANALYSIS,

By PROF. C. F. CHANDLER, of the Columbia School of Mines.

Solid contents of one gallon, of 231 cubic inches:

Chloride of Sodium	328.468	grains.
Chloride of Potassium	8.327	"
Bromide of Sodium	.414	"
Iodide of Sodium	.066	"
Fluoride of Calcium	trace	"
Bicarbonate of Lithia	4.326	"
Bicarbonate of Soda	10.064	"
Bicarbonate of Magnesia	75.161	"
Bicarbonate of Lime	101.881	"
Bicarbonate of Strontia	trace	"
Bicarbonate of Baryta	.726	"
Bicarbonate of Iron	2.038	"
Sulphate of Potassa	2.158	"
Phosphate of Soda	.009	"
Biborate of Soda	trace	"
Alumina	·305	"
Silica	3.213	"
Organic matter	trace	"
Sulphur,		
Total	537.155	"
Carbonic Acid Gas	317.452	cubic inches.
Density	1.006	
Temperature	.45°F.	

From Dr. Bedortha.

"This valuable Spring adds new attractions to invalids and to all who visit Saratoga. The waters are highly medicinal and equal to the best springs of the place. They are *cathartic* and *tonic*, containing, as is seen, iron and sulphur, very useful in dyspepsia, constipation, kidney complaints, scrofula, skin diseases, rheumatism, &c., and a cooling and refreshing beverage."

N. BEDORTHA, M. D.

ANALYSIS

OF THE

RED SPRING.

The following analysis of *Red Spring* water was made by Prof. JOHN H. APPLETON, of Brown University, Providence, R. I. The amounts specify the number of grains of the various substances in one Imperial gallon of the water:

Bicarbonate of Lithia	$LiO,HO\ 2\ CO_2$,	.242	grains.
Bicarbonate of Soda,	$NaO,HO\ 2\ CO_2$,	15.327	"
Bicarbonate of Magnesia,	$MgO,HO\ 2\ CO_2$,	42.413	"
Bicarbonate of Lime	$CaO,HO\ 2\ CO_2$,	101.256	"
Cloride of Sodium,	Na Cl,	83.530	"
Chloride of Potassium	K Cl,	6.587	"
Alumina and Sesquioxide of Iron		2.100	"
Silica		3.255	"
Phosphates		a trace.	
		254.710	"

We present above the analysis, one of the most careful and complete examinations ever made, and showing the presence, in great abundance, of those elements which constitute the value of all mineral springs. The effect of this water as an alterative is far superior to that of any other spring, and so great that small quantities produce the desired results, making it, thereby, wonderfully suited to the weakest stomachs, in cases of long and extreme chronic disease. This quality of the water is due to the peculiar combination of its ingredients. We revert only to the fact which every chemist knows, that a slight change in its elements often converts a *deadly poison* into a nutritious food or a powerful medicine.

Dr. Steel spoke of the wonderful power of this water in curing Salt Rheum and skin diseases, nearly fifty years ago, in a little work he wrote on the character of "Our MINERAL SPRINGS."

For particulars of the many cures by the use of this water, call for a circular, at the bottling-house of the RED SPRING, on Spring avenue.

STAR SPRING CO.,

SARATOGA, N. Y.

For a period of over half a century, the water of this spring has been favorably known to the citizens and visitors of Saratoga, and yet it was not until 1862 that its real merits were fully developed. Owing to the great amount of *Iodine* with which the water is charged, it was always held in high esteem by invalids, and especially those suffering from Chronic Rheumatism, Scrofulous complaints, Cutaneous Eruptions, &c.

An Analysis of the water was soon after made by Professor CHANDLER, which demonstrated conclusively, that, in wealth of mineral matter, it far surpasses any of the other fountains of Saratoga. Containing every ingredient found in the other springs in a much larger amount, it likewise is impregnated with several salts, not shown in the analysis of other springs of the place. As a *Beverage* it has no superior; as a *Cathartic* it is unsurpassed, and as a Tonic and Diuretic it is second to none yet discovered.

In view of the facts stated, it is claimed that the Star water will secure:

1st. All the benefits or advantages that can be derived from the use of any other of the waters of Saratoga.

2d. That it is vastly superior to any other in the treatment of diseases where the use of Iodine is desirable.

3d. That, owing to the greater quantity of Carbonic Acid Gas with which it is charged, it will preserve better and longer, bottled, than any other now known.

4th. That there is no natural mineral fountain in Saratoga, nor in the *world*, as yet known to science, that is so richly charged with health giving and health preserving properties.

Price of quarts, per dozen (2 doz. in case), - - - -	$2.50
Per Gross, - - - - - - - - - - - - -	30.00
Pints, per dozen (4 doz. in case), - - - - - - -	1.75
Per Gross, - - - - - - - - - - - - -	21.00
Thirty gallon bbls., - - - - - - - - - - -	23.50

Water 20 cents per gallon in bulk; customers paying the freight on the empty casks to Saratoga and full ones back.

TERMS CASH.

ADDRESS—*Star Spring Co., Saratoga Springs, N. Y.*

"GEYSER OR SPOUTING SPRING."

HATHORN SPRING.

H. H. HATHORN, - - - : - - - - - - *Proprietor.*

CONGRESS HALL,

H. H. HATHORN & CO., Proprietors.

www.ingramcontent.com/pod-product-compliance
Lightning Source LLC
Chambersburg PA
CBHW021528270326
41930CB00008B/1148

* 9 7 8 3 3 3 7 4 1 7 7 1 0 *